THE MARKETING SNITCH
The Book Marketing Gurus
Don't Want You To Read!

by

Anonymous Snitch

For more information:
info@themarketingsnitch.com

ISBN- 9781699022405

Book cover by Stevano Vicigor

CONTENTS

DISCLAIMER

I wrote this book anonymously because I knew it would offend some people. I wanted to *"rat out"* the information that so called self proclaimed gurus are passing out. I use the word gurus throughout this book to describe self proclaimed internet marketers or self improvement individuals who are giving rookies and veteran marketers wrong or not enough information needed to generate internet sales.

If you're in business you need marketing more than ever and there are people who will take advantage of that fact and will sell you everything you *don't need*. The words in this book are my opinions based on my marketing journey.

I'm not saying the information you will read in this book is the holy grail of marketing, however the hundreds of hours I put into understanding marketing has given me a marketing self education degree. I hope the information will be useful to you in your plight to earn money on and off the internet because why else would you care about marketing?

INTRODUCTION

No Marketing Guru Is Going To Save You

Nobody but you will save you from yourself. No one is going to come into your life with all the answers. No one is going to do the hard work you need to do to become a success in your life. You will not have a lifeboat waiting to take you to the next level of your life. Nobody is coming to save you.

So take out your cheerleader tassels and root for yourself. Be the loudest cheerleader ever for you. You want that pat on the back then pat yourself. Do you need someone to tell you that you look great? Then look in the mirror and tell yourself you look marvelous!

Do you need someone to tell you that you're doing a great job? Tell yourself you're doing a fantastic job no matter how small the job might be. A job could be as simple as mopping the floor in your home.

Are you waiting on a like or a clap to validate how good you write, spell or convey your message to the market? Don't wait any longer, validate yourself by telling yourself in the mirror, eye to eye that you don't need a freakin' "clap," a "like" or an "endorsement" from anyone to know how great you are! You have to clap, like and endorse yourself daily with a pat on the back.

No more letting others have control of how you feel about yourself. No more relying on TV, Facebook, Instagram, Twitter, Youtube, or any other social platform to say how wonderful and talented you are. You are who you are without any apologies to anyone.

You are the most powerful person that you know. Yes, You! No need to compare yourself to others and what they got. No need to wish you were like someone else. Be proud of who you are and grateful that you can recognize the Good and Beauty in yourself.

Life is too short to feel sorry for you. Life is too short for you not to believe in yourself. The old saying is true, *"believe in yourself and others will believe in you."* No need to say you "can't" do something when it's just as easy to say you "can." No more self-pity parties you are bigger than that. Know that you have what it takes to be and do whatever you want to do.

If you don't know what you are supposed to do, then you need to ask your brain-computer questions, and you will get the answers. Your brain-computer might give you answers that you don't agree with, but at least look at what your brain-computer feeds back to you.

When you ask your brain-computer questions, it goes into the hard drive of your mind and brings you answers based on your experiences and what you have picked up by others in your life. Don't argue with your conscious *mind* what the brain-computer *(sub conscious mind)* feeds back to you. Just analyze the feedback.

You have bigger fish to fry then what's happening in your life now, and you know this! I bet you want to inspire others. I bet you're a leader beneath your calm style. I bet you want to write a book or books about what you know. I bet you are passionate. I bet you know that you can make a difference on planet earth. I bet you **believe** you deserve recognition for being the best at what you do.

Nobody is coming to save you but you, so put yourself in a lifeboat and get paddling towards the success that you know is destined for you—whatever that *"success"* is to you…. and *I can assure you that whatever you do Marketing is the missing link.*

YOU ARE BEING LIED TO!

I wrote this book as a warning to marketing rookies and veterans looking to make money on the internet. I want to warn you about getting caught up and spending money on books, audio recordings, webinars, seminars, workshops, stats, advertising, promoting and still not making any money.

You keep *searching* because you believe in yourself. You won't and can't quit, but you know time is passing you by and you still aren't making any cash. You've been attracted to various shiny objects and now your bank account is close to zero. What do I suggest? **Marketing!**

The key is to understand what marketing really is and why you need it. Already, more than 57,000+ internet marketers in the USA alone – *rookies and pros alike* – have been tricked, fooled and are being charged thousands and maybe millions of dollars for bogus marketing information!

I'm Not Hatin'

…on anyone, but I have hundreds of hours reading books, listening to audio, watching videos and writing about marketing and I'd like to think I have an opinion on the subject.

There are some bad marketers on the internet and I call them *marketing gangsters*. They get money from uniformed entrepreneurs and business people but have never marketed any products or services themselves, and will shoot down other marketers with their insecure mouths. Some are self proclaimed guru's who make their money copying real marketers with a track record.

I've come to realize **the gurus that are telling you how and what to do to make money don't do it themselves**. They've figured the way to make money off people is to sell them on **"how to make money on the internet"** and it's usually in the form of a book, video or audio recording.

ARE GURUS MAKING MONEY?

Of course! Think of all those gullible people losing their hard earned cash and you don't want to be gullible do you? I'm envious of the money I know some guru's are earning, but they put in the work and deserve the money right? I say no! Some of the self proclaimed gurus are nothing more than copy cats of those that have done the real work.

I'm not gonna lie, I was jealous a few times of all the money a few gurus earned in a short period of time. I'm talking about verified millions! I know because they bragged about it or I was a part of their group. Besides you hear them talk about expensive houses, and cars with fat bank accounts. Whether it's true or not (*I say it's not true for some of them*) they trick people into buying marketing products from them.

Can You Make Money On The Internet?

That's the bottom line question people ask. The answer is **Yes! Loads of it!** So what are the guru's secrets? Selling people on *"how"'* to make money on the internet. It's as simple as that.

I don't make all my money teaching others how to make money *(I actually run real business)* so because of that, it doesn't hurt me to share with you what I know. I get so irritated with so called gurus tossing out bogus numbers and stats without any real proof to back it up.

So how do you make money from the internet? You have to read *(self education)*, learn any skills necessary, put into action what you learn, and strategize the marketing of products or services that *people want* and *not what they need.* If strategizing a marketing plan is not for you it's ok to hire someone, but they must give you the real and tested numbers of your marketing campaign.

Tell the gurus you want to see the proof in real time. Or else don't waste your time, money or energy in a marketing strategy unless you get the highest probability of success, in the shortest time, with minimal effort.

WHAT'S MARKETING ANYWAY?

MY definition of marketing is "pre-selling" a product or service to prospective buyers, so when they contact the seller they are ready to buy. Think of it like this, you have a fast racing car you want to sell. You place a classified ad in a local newspaper so this would be called **advertising.** Then you race the car around town with for sale signs on both sides. This would be called **promotion** or promoting the sale of the race car.

A couple of neighborhood goons steal the race car and after a high speed chase end up in jail. The local news reported the incident live on TV. This would be called **publicity.** A rookie reporter interviews the seller of the race car after the criminals were arrested. This would be called **public relations.**

A news viewer saw the cop chase and immediately contacted the seller and bought the car. This would be the **sale** of the race car which was the sellers intention.

All these events were used in **marketing** the sale of the race car even if some of the events were unplanned. If you can understand the sequence of events that lead up to the sale of the race car, you will understand *Marketing!*

WHAT'S A VALUE LADDER?

A value ladder is a method of mapping out your product or service offer visually in ascending order of value and price. To understand a value ladder more below is an example of a dentist value ladder.

This ladder bugs me because I see my dentist using a value ladder and makes me wonder if I truly need the extra services. Have you ever seen this value ladder? The gurus use one all the time when they give you a free ebook or download.

Then you'll get a few chummy emails in which they will try to up sell you to something more profitable so don't fall for it. Don't they know we are hip to their game? Many business owners and entrepreneurs don't know about the value ladder they just "up sale" without being consciously aware of what they are doing. You want fries with that Big Mac sir?

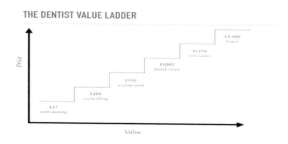

THE DENTIST VALUE LADDER

© 2019 themarketingsnitch.com

WHAT'S SEO AND IS IT IMPORTANT?

Search engine optimization is what it's called and is the process of increasing the **quality** and **quantity** of website traffic by increasing the **visibility** of a website or a web page to users of a web search engine like Google.

In the simplest terms you use *keywords* to define how browsers like Google, Internet Explorer and Safari will find your website. Gurus would have you think that SEO is some complicated acronym that you can't understand and need to pay them for services.

SEO is important because on the internet you are competing with other websites that want your buyers and keywords are the key to optimizing Google and other browsers like Yahoo and Bing to find what customers need.

The gurus won't give you the best keywords because you will be in competition with them.

Secret tip to more traffic: targeted specific keywords and keywords phrases.

KEYWORDS
(THE SECRET)

Keywords go hand and hand with SEO and gurus aren't going to give you all the best keywords because you would be in competition with them.

A **keyword** is a word used to describe something buyers are searching for on Google, Amazon or even Facebook. Most people type in a **keyword phrase** to narrow their search for what they want. An example would be a search for "*organic bananas*" and you would get websites that sell organic bananas. Keywords are important as that's how your website will get traffic.

Secret tip: Add the keywords money, job, work, Facebook, Google, money, education and Amazon to your website or your marketing strategy and see what happens. Your traffic will explode! You might not convert everyone, but you will see an increase in your stats.

Wordstream.com is free keyword tool so give it a try before you a pay a guru a few hundred for some bogus keywords.

What's Page Ranking and Does it Matter?

Ranking refers to the process search engines use to determine where a particular piece of content should appear on a Google Search Engine Results Page *(SERP)*. Or simply put when you type in a search for something you are looking for, the first Google page you see would be the highest ranking page and the first website on that page would rank #1.

Gurus would have you believe you need to rank number one on a Google search to get website traffic and most of the time you won't need to. The key are the *"words"* on your website and the users who type in those words or a variation of words that will rank you higher.

If you are selling purple polka dotted pants you will rank high on a Google search page because of the unique words you are using. So when a marketing guru tells you they can rank you high on Google just yawn and tell him to keep walking because you can rank 50 and still get traffic.

WHAT'S A SALES FUNNEL?

The sales funnel refers to the buying process that companies lead customers through when purchasing products or services. The definition also refers to the process through which a company finds, qualifies, and sells its products or services to buyers.

The typical sales funnel is divided into multiple steps, which differ depending on the sales model. A sales funnel allows you to cultivate leads into customers over time. To put it simply, the funnel provides you with the sales process you need to convert unaware consumers into paying customers. Most gurus put you through this sales funnel process.

What Happens in Your Sales Funnel?

© 2019 themarketingsnitch.com

They literally have you go thru a maze like a little rat. Some have at least five maze gates to go through to purchase their products. Behind the scenes they can see your every move on their website and will promptly send you an email if you don't buy something.

There's a lot of misinformation about sales funnels and rookies and veteran marketers are confused with information overload. Sales funnels are great but if you don't have one doesn't mean you can get new costumers.

Gurus automate the process with some combination of lead magnets, emails, webinars, and sales letters so these freebies will do the selling for them.

Gurus promise sales funnels work and will work for you. They preach you need Facebook ads, automated webinars, and complicated sales funnel sequences to build a business that makes money and it's not true.

The only thing that's going to make money for you is marketing a product or service the consumers want. So your job is to teach yourself marketing and stop spending all your money on shinny objects, because you can learn marketing practically free.

FACEBOOK ADS WHY YOU SHOULD ADVERTISE

Most small businesses and entrepreneurs don't know the power of Facebook ads. They know there are advertising opportunities on Facebook, but don't know how to tap into them. Facebook knows everything about its members which results in better target marketing.

However, gurus won't tell you that Facebook is useless unless you have an effective landing page or website. They will take your Facebook budget of thousands but will not update your website.

Gurus don't tell you that Facebook is good at generating leads. What they do is sale you on the fact the ads are cheap and depends largely on your ability to build an audience.

Gurus don't tell you about your Facebook ads getting kicked back if you used words like "you" and "your" in your ad campaign. This is important because most business people use those words.

Gurus don't tell you that people on Facebook don't really care about your products. They're there to check out family photos and reading about gossip. This means if a guru is saying sell sell sell to FB people you know they're a rookie.

Gurus don't tell you to avoid negative words like diet, weight loss, fat, depression, anxiety, stress, fear, overwhelm, and terrified is because they don't know they are violating FB rules. Keep this in mind when you advertise on FB.

Gurus don't tell you that FB doesn't like get rich quick money making scams or work-from-home ads. So don't market your product or service like an old school used car salesman.

Most of all, **gurus** don't tell you that FB not only checks your ads but also your landing page and your website for bad language, scams and fraudulent activity.

Facebook ads open up a world of opportunity if used correctly, so make sure your **guru** knows what he or she is doing or you will spend thousands and most of it will go in the bank accounts they brag about.

WHY YOU SHOULD USE GOOGLE ADWORDS

Google Adwords is an online advertising platform developed by Google. The program allows you to create online ads to reach audiences that are interested in the products and services you offer. Advertisers pay to display their ads which can be YouTube videos, gmail ads, banners or mobile ads to web users.

Google ads when done right can increase leads, website traffic, target users, and brand recognition. I use Google Adwords for website traffic and I've paid as low as .50 per day and a penny for an ad. I know it sounds crazy but if you want to quickly add 10,000 hits to your YouTube channel Google Adwords is the way to go.

Thus you can use Google Adwords to get leads and sales from customer searches. You can advertise on YouTube or send your ads directly into the email box of thousands and perhaps millions of gmail users.

Also in order to use Google Adwords you need a gmail account.

YOUTUBE ADS AND WHY YOU SHOULD ADVERTISE

Most Google Adwords ads run on Youtube, on Google Search or sent directly to Google gmail email accounts. These ads can be incredibly cheap; however gurus will tell you to spend thousands of dollars. I'm telling you now that gurus make money off YouTube ads by not showing their clients the true stats.

Gurus that are good with Adwords simply won't show you the real numbers. They'll make it seem like Google Adwords is mind boggling to figure it out, but don't listen to them; demand to see your stats in real time. Gurus can take $1,000 of your hard earned cash and give you 5,000 YouTube views to show the ads are getting visits or hits, but in actuality it may have only cost them $200 thus making $800 profit off of you.

Understand what your results mean and don't let gurus tell you that you need thousands of dollars for a YouTube ad campaign because you can have a decent campaign with $200! I know I focused on the views, but the quality of engagement is more important than the number of views as this will make a difference in YouTube rankings.

Cost Per Click (CPC)

CPC aka pay-per-click (PPC) is the actual rate you pay for each click in your marketing campaigns. An advertiser pays Google *(as an example)* when the ad is clicked.

You should focus on what really matters when it comes to your marketing campaign, which is cost per sale. Exactly how much are you spending to get people to buy your product or service? Cost per sale is really the bottom line when it comes to CPC.

According to WordStream, the average cost per click on the search networks across all industries is $2.32, but gurus will tell you it's much higher to pad their pockets when I've personally have paid as low as .01 CPC.

Remember you always want to see your numbers in real time. Do not allow the guru to send you an excel worksheet or pdf report that can be altered to fit their budget not yours.

If you have a high CPC and no conversions meaning nobody bought anything from you it's time to re-evaluate your marketing campaign or give your guru the boot.

WHY YOU SHOULD BE AWARE

Some gurus think buyers are **suckers**. They will show their beautiful leased homes and expensive leased cars and flash duplicate $100 bills, not caring that the buyer is seeing all of that and feeling like a fool.

You should be aware of gurus who make absolute promises they can't keep. You should be aware that you don't have to spend thousands of dollars to get good marketing results. If you don't do your own marketing and want to hire a guru *(a self proclaimed internet marketer)* make sure they are testing your marketing campaign.

You should be aware of any guru who doesn't test your marketing campaign because you will be throwing money out the window if you don't. You can test your marketing campaigns by gender, age, zip code, likes, country, income and more! Thank you Facebook and Google!

Make these gurus earn their money!

FAKE EXPERTS, PHONIES AND FLAKES

Most of the younger gurus who haven't put in the time, copied the info from the older guru's and re-packaged it for their markets. Repackaged gurus have copied the old greats like Napoleon Hill, Jim Rohn, Gary Halbert, David Ogilvy and others. You can tell who's a copy cat because they're repeating the words of the greats.

I'm not saying Bob Proctor or Anthony Robbins and others like them are copy cats because they'd say those they followed were their mentors. Nor am I saying they're fakes or phonies. It's clear that Bob Proctor utilizes the work of Napoleon Hill to get rich and Anthony Robbins used the work of Jim Rohn to get rich as others have.

The fake experts and phonies that I'm talking about are the arm chair marketers that make money copying and compiling information from around the internet and selling it to rookie and veteran marketers.

How do you know who's a fake expert, phony or a flake? You don't….

They're Laughing At You

Because you don't know what you're doing. The gurus laugh right in your face telling you how much money they're earning off their sales that includes you, but you still buy from them. No worries they got me too.

You have to be careful in the marketing game because you will be attracted to every *"shiny new thing."* You'll get caught up with books, audio recordings, webinars, seminars, workshops, YouTube videos, stats, advertising, and promotions thinking you need to become a social media top dog to feed the edge you feel to make cash.

It's ok to want to know it all, just don't reinvent the wheel. At the end of this book I mention some of the gurus you should check out to get you started on the right path and some you should pass by...

THEIR HOUSES AND CARS ARE LEASED

Since gurus are always displaying their wealth I can assure you're their **mansions, houses and cars are leased.** Because of my background with bookkeeping and taxes they would be advised by their expensive CPA's to lease and not buy anything.

They would be a fool to buy mansions and exotic cars because the market is too flexible and their wealth could be gone overnight and besides it's not smart to *buy* certain items when you make a lot of cash.

Doing The Math - I can do the math. If a guru has a webinar, seminar, workshop or master mind, most of them will have a Facebook group. So if you multiply the member's times the amount the guru charged for the event you can to an idea of how much they earned.

Also gurus can't help but boast about how much they earn as well.

What Do I Suggest?

Take the Kolby.com test. I'll talk more on this in a minute, but in a nutshell you'll find out where you stand as far as what type of person you are. Not an IQ or personality test, but a *"who you are test"* and will definitely help you with your life choices. This self knowledge will also help you with the marketing process.

You don't know what you don't know. I didn't understand that phrase when I first heard it. And it's true, you don't know what you don't know until you cross the path of what it is you are supposed to know, then you get it and have a *ah ha moment.*

There are lots of books, YouTube videos and podcasts to listen to and some of them are a complete waste of time. However, coming up next is a short list of the top books, videos and websites that have helped and *hindered me* with self improvement and marketing as the two go hand in hand.

If you are not confident, how can you sell your products or services, let alone someone else's?

MARKETS WORTH TARGETING
Below are niches on the rise

- ✓ Health and Wellness
- ✓ Dating and Relationships
- ✓ Hobbies
- ✓ Beauty and Fashion
- ✓ Pets
- ✓ Outdoor survival
- ✓ Loans
- ✓ Investments
- ✓ Languages
- ✓ Travel
- ✓ Self-Improvement
- ✓ Wealth building
- ✓ Home decor and DIY
- ✓ Gadgets and Technology
- ✓ Personal Finance
- ✓ **Affiliate marketing**
- ✓ Make Money on the Internet
- ✓ Fitness
- ✓ Weight Loss (*P90X, Weight Watchers, the Atkins Diet, the South Beach Diet, and the Keto Diet are the most popular weight loss products*)

If you don't have a product or service pick a niche above and get to work!

Reviews of Marketing and Self Improvement Gurus

I mentioned that self improvement and marketing go hand in hand. Think about it, if you are marketing your product or service you have to have a certain level of confidence wouldn't you agree?

- People buy from confident people not from people who don't know WTF is going on wouldn't you agree?
- You want to learn something if you are going to take the time to read it, watch it or listen to it right?

I labeled the following gurus as either a **reporter or expert** in their field. This is a short list of many gurus and I know many great ones are missing…

Reporters interview gurus and entrepreneurs and then feeds it to their audience via a book, video or audio recording. **Experts** teach what they know and the student listens. Experts are great ways to quantum leap your knowledge and success.

The following reviews are my opinions of marketing and self improvement gurus and are based on my interactions with them…*again this is not all of them…*

Kathy Kolbe.com - *Expert/Reporter*

Before you do anything take this $55 dollar 36 question test created by Kathy Kolbe. It's not a personality or an IQ test but a test that measures who you are naturally.

Above are my numbers and tells a lot about me which is a book in its self, but when I really understood the numbers and why I operate the way I do, it has literally changed the navigation of my life.

I highly recommend you finding out how you *operate*. This test can save you time and heartache…it will also help you to understand the direction you should take in your life.

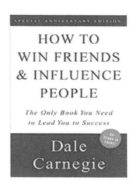

Dale Carnegie *(RIP) - Expert*

I highly recommend you read this book in the beginning of your journey if you are going to make money on or off line. In order to make money you have to deal with people.

    "How To Win Friends & Influence People" will make you a better person in your personal and business life. I know it's an old book but the information is too important to miss so just read it!

Gary Halbert *(RIP) - Expert*

I didn't know about copywriting until I heard Russell Brunson mention Gary Halbert. I Goggled him and found a gold mine of information about copywriting and a true understanding of what marketing is about.

I was introduced to the **"Sales Letter."** They call it copywriting. I've heard of copywriting but I saw *copy writing as* legalizing my work but what I'm typing right now is considered *copy.*

Visit Gary's website and gobble up all the valuable information available. Don't worry about the age of the content as it's timeless and will set you on the right path.

I like Gary but it seems he became a marketing gangster as he figured out a way to get lots of money out of people. He was too wise for his own good. I'll recommend his work but sometimes seems he comes off as an egotistical sleazebag. www.thegaryhalbertletter.com

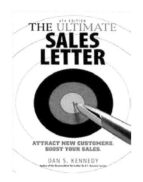

Dan Kennedy *(RIP 2019) - Expert*

I ran across Dan while listening to Joe Polish who was talking about Gary Halbert. Dan takes the sales letter to the next level in his book **"*The Ultimate Sales Letter.*"** I really enjoyed this book and the examples Dan gave. This book is from the 90's but the information is still relevant and a must read to get you ready for marketing.

Dan is good but can come off as an arrogant used car salesman but his books are worth reading along with his YouTube videos.

Allan Dib - *Expert*

I just ran across Allan recently and although he takes some of his words from other authors he brings it all together in his simplistic book **"The 1-Page Marketing Plan."** This e-book was full of gems that I quickly implemented into my marketing plan. I highly recommend reading this book in the beginning of your journey and when you get to the even deeper stuff it will make more sense.

Joe Polish - *Reporter/Expert*

I like Joe. I found out about Joe while watching a Gary Halbert video. So I searched out Joe and found a video of him giving props to Gary Halbert while displaying a brilliant marketing strategy. I saw him get a crowd of hundreds of people to buy his product @ $500 a pop. It was pure genius!

There's more to Joe since that first video and his website is a must to understanding marketing www.ilovemarketing.com. I suggest you watch or listen to all the videos and podcasts from the very LAST video to the first video. Your head will explode with knowledge!

Dean Jackson - *Reporter/Expert* - Dean has a podcast with Joe Polish and has some great thoughts too. I particularly liked the *"focus finder"* video that gives great insight on putting your business life in order. This info in the beginning of your marketing journey is important as it will help navigate your time in the most efficient way.

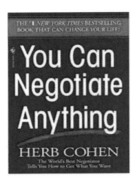

Herb Cohen - *Expert*

I like Herb and when I found out he was a lawyer I understood why his book was on *"negotiating."* That's why you need to read his book *"You Can Negotiate Anything."* Don't listen to the audio because you won't get the full effect of what he's saying. You need the book so you can underline all the gems that will help you get more out of your life and people.

Every day we are negotiating something and when it comes to marketing negotiating is at the top of the list. Whether it's negotiating a deal with the web designer or a guru for their services, you need to know how to negotiate and when to spot it when it's happening to you. Herb is an entertaining writer and I highly recommend this book!

© 2019 themarketingsnitch.com

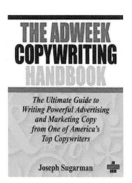

Joe Sugarman - *Expert*

I like Joe he comes from a different perspective. He's a self made man who's mastered the art of writing spectacular sales letters and copy. The word *"copy"* doesn't mean a copy you make on a machine. Copy is what you are reading now, my words.

I never knew that and want you to know it. It's important in business and in life to be able to persuade people with your words and to make them think they thought of it. I like Joe's mind and his marketing strategies. This book is a must read to get your creative marketing juices flowing!

David Ogilvy *(RIP) - Expert*

I like David's bold attitude. His book on advertising and copywriting helped me understand the print layout and how to grab the reader's attention. He uses cool ideas to get his points across and is a guru worth reading. His books are full of gems and I highly recommend as you try to understand marketing and advertising.

I like David but he was egotistical and self centered… which I guess is a good thing when it comes to marketing.

Success Secrets TV - *Expert*

These YouTube videos are fabulous and a must view. Take the time to watch at least 2 hours worth and take notes because this channel is dropping real gems with most of the videos about 10 minutes long.

SST has almost 600 videos that you can learn from. Take the time to watch 25 of them and it will change your world view. Search "Success Secrets TV" on Youtube and open the door to summaries of hundreds of books and thoughts on those books. I highly recommend these videos!

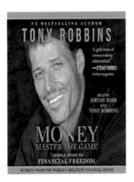

Anthony Robbins - *Expert*

I remember Anthony when he came on the scene *(I still have his personal power cassette tapes)* he was and still is a powerhouse of energy. His style is about doing it now and being aggressive. He has plenty of gems and is heavily into self improvement which is why he's so great. I like Anthony but he's egotistical and talks too much, however you can learn a lot from him and I highly recommend his videos and books.

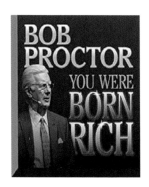

Bob Proctor - *Expert*

I resonated with Bob when I first ran across his videos and his talk about money. I even went to his Paradigm Shift seminar. I really liked his terror barrier philosophy meaning when our minds try to hold us back recognize it and go around it. Bob is about self improvement and making money. He's convinced his followers that repetitive content is the key to riches and apparently so with his fat wallet and lovely house in Arizona.

His followers will say the seminar is about getting together, but I've been to the seminar and I don't see a need to keep paying for the exact same information and people. I call it mind control because of the repetitive nature and because of the cash pouring into The Proctor-Gallagher pockets. Go to the seminars if you must, otherwise view Bob's YouTube videos.

Darren Hardy - *Expert*

I like Darrin and the discipline he brings to the table. He has a way to get you up and moving. His positive energy and words are inspiring when you need a lift. He's a self improvement guy but you can learn so much more about time management, reaching goals and taking life one step at a time. I highly recommend his books and watching his YouTube videos.

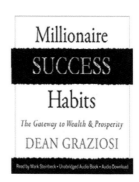

Dean Graziosi – *Expert*

I like Dean, he over delivers. He's into self improvement and teaming up with others to show you the full package from self improvement to marketing. I like his style and high energy.

He teamed up with Anthony Robbins and Russell Brunson for a Master Mind I'm a part of. The group earned $30 million in less than 3 months! I know because I did the math plus they got $2,500 from me. It was worth every penny! It's called the KBB Blue Print Master Mind and comes at $2,000-$2,500 a pop!

Dean has been around for awhile and has numerous books and videos. He talks quite a bit but that's ok because he's dropping knowledge. I highly recommend his work.

Evan Carmichael - *Reporter*

I like Evan's YouTube channel. He's also written a couple of books. His reporter style is a breath of fresh air as he interviews entrepreneurs of all walks of life.

I like his top 10 rules for success that he gets from movers and shakers on the planet. I highly recommend his YouTube channel. *Search "Evan Carmichael" on YouTube.*

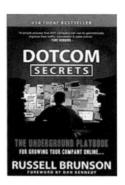

Russell Brunson - *Expert*

I like Russell. I need to finish his book "Dotcom Secrets." There's so much information that I started taking action before I read the whole book. I didn't know about *"funnels"* and had an eye opener with Russell's book.

It was because of Russell I found Gary Halbert and was introduced to direct mail marketing. Russell writes about the *"value ladder"* that I didn't know about. It's like you go to the dentist based on a free ad for dental cleaning then up the value ladder you go, from a cleaning to a root canal to a crown spending big money.

This info bugged me because I can see the "value ladder" in almost every industry. I recommend this book to learn about the value ladder and other internet marketing secrets.

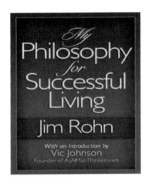

Jim Rohn *(RIP)* Expert

I have been into self improvement for years, but Jim Rohn woke me back up to the importance of self education. Jim is a must to make sure you keep your journey on the right track. I highly recommend Jim's communication videos on YouTube as they are life savers along with his great books.

Neil Patel.com - *Expert*

I like Neil and his free marketing information. He gets into detail regarding content, search engine optimization and conversions. I've learned a lot from Neil but haven't earned any money with his ideas, but I guess it's not his fault. I would say watch his videos and listen to his podcast to learn what you can. I would also say subscribe to his mailing list.

Sometimes there's a discrepancy in his information so I don't rely too much on his words.

Tai Lopez.com - *Expert*

I liked Tai when I first ran across his YouTube videos. He was the first person I paid money to after seeing a YouTube video of him looking like he just woke up. His mansion and cars had me thinking he was making big cash *(and I'm sure he has)*; however I soon saw that he was making money by telling others how to make money, knowing 90% of the people would never make any.

I soon grew tired of him bragging about all his riches and denounced my membership that took a threat to get out of. I can't recommend Tai at this time.

No One Gets It Right
The First Time

There are other writers with great information out there but the previous books and videos helped me and had I read and watched them first my journey would have been less rocky, but then again I learned while in the process so it's a win win situation.

Procrastination - Is the one single reason that most people fail. *"I'll do it when the kids get out of school, I'll do it when the kids go to college, I'll do it when I retire,"* and guess what you never do it. Life can be brutal when you waste time! Do it now!

Experimenting - No one knows how to become successful until they try. Bill Gates, Steve Jobs, Elon Musk, Oprah and numerous others did not know they would be where they are or how big they were going to be unless they tried.

No gets it right - No one starts out with everything set up for them. You won't have all the resources you need, but you must start anyway.

It takes time to achieve anything and this is a true saying and one I had to learn the hard way. I always thought I could knock a product or service out of the park sort of like people who think they'll hit the lottery on the first try.

The journey to success is a long walk that never ends, so don't procrastinate or you'll wake up one day wondering where all your time went. The time is never right for you to begin; you just begin where ever you are…

I wrote this book hoping to help alleviate some of your pain while searching the internet to find a solution to your marketing and financial woes. I wrote this book so you don't get trapped into buying every shiny thing in regards to marketing. Just remember…

Gurus make money telling other people how to make money whether they've made any money or not.

It's time to educate yourself and let the world know who you are *(even if you don't want to)* and marketing is the key. As I said in the beginning, if you really want to make money on the internet you must do one or all of the following: write a book *(ebooks count)*, create a video *(or film)* or record audio *(includes music and audio books)*.

You can teach people how to make money within your industry on the internet or copy other gurus because that's what most of them did.

The Offer is the Secret

No matter what a guru says and no matter what your product or service, it all boils down to the offer. What are you offering if I purchase your product or service?

What do I get if I buy from you?

- Am I going to get something free with the purchase?
- Am I going to get something additional with the purchase?
- Am I going to get a free ebook (s)?
- Am I going to get a guarantee or discount?
- Am I going to get free shipping?

This book is an example. If you buy the book you can have the Kindle free. I would love to add a t-shirt or give an additional discount, maybe a free car, but if I do I would be at a loss. So the seller can only go so far or be broke.

Whatever your product or service, **the offer is the main key to the sale.** Obviously it would be nice to have a great product or service and even a decent website.

Just remember, try to give the best offer you possibly can and if they still don't buy, they never were.

INTERNET MARKETING TERMS YOU SHOULD KNOW

Affiliate marketing - Selling your product or service through other websites, individuals and e-mail lists or it's a great way to make money referring buyers to sellers of products or services.

Analytics - Analyzing your website traffic and then making adjustments to get better results.

Blog - Writers publish short stories, articles, events, upload pictures and information on a regular basis and let visitors post comments and likes.

Conversion rate - The number of sales. Period.

Domain name - The address of your web site, such as Amazon.com.

Page view - If I visit your web site and look at 3 pages, that will count as 3 page views.

Ping - Means notifying the world that you've updated your web site.

PPC - Pay per click is a great way to generate business fast, or spend a small fortune and get no return at all.

Ranking - Determines how you rank for a specific keyword in search engines.

RSS - A file that delivers a list of headlines and content directly to a subscriber's inbox

Search Engine - Google, Yahoo, Internet Explorer, Safari and Bing are examples of search engines.

SEO - *(Search Engine Optimization)* with the right keywords on your web site you will get high ranking thus more potential customers.

Spam - Unsolicited e-mail, negative comments, repeated submissions to blogs and discussion forums.

URL - (*Uniform Resource Locator)* your unique website address like Amazon.com.

Unique visitor - If I come to your web site 20 times in a month, I still only count as one unique visitor.

Visit - Any user visiting your site any one time.

Remember, marketing is the key to everything you want to do and must be the focal point!

Go get 'em!

I'd love to tell you who I am but that's not important, however your feedback is important so give me a review on Amazon good or bad!

Thank you!

Good luck and keep educating yourself!

Anonymous Snitch

Printed in Great Britain
by Amazon

38497392R00033